The River Tamar

Sarah Foot

GW00384282

BOSSINEY BOOKS

First published in 1989 by
Bossiney Books
St Teath, Bodmin, Cornwall.

Typeset and Printed by
Clowes Book Printers
St Columb, Cornwall.

Bound by R Booth (Bookbinders) Ltd
Mabe Burnthouse, Cornwall

PLATE ACKNOWLEDGMENTS
Cover photography by Andrew Besley and
The National Trust
Back cover by Ray Bishop
Ray Bishop: pages 3, 6, 9, 11, 13,
17, 20, 21, 25, 27, 28, 31, 43, 44, 48,
49, 53, 65, 67, 68, 69, 71, 72, 77,
89, 90.
Alice Boyd: pages 39, 61, 83.
Morwellham Quay: pages 53, 49, 54.
Sheila Lightbody: page 56.
Bob Wellard: pages 32, 35, 36, 41.

Netting for salmon in the River Tamar near Cotehele.

About the author
and the book

Sarah Foot has a passion for rivers. She lives in a beautiful converted barn at Elmgate, overlooking the River Lynher. Formerly on the staff of the 'London Evening News', Sarah Foot has written on a wide range of Westcountry subjects in the last decade for the Western Morning News and the Sunday Independent. She is the Editor of Cornish Scene, a quarterly devoted to Cornwall and Cornish causes.

This is her ninth title for Bossiney. The River Tamar is an enlarged and up-dated version of Following the Tamar, first published in 1980.

Here she traces the great river from its beginnings on the North Cornish coast all the way down to Brunel's historic bridge. Tamar lakes and Bude canal, Launceston and Lifton, Calstock and Cotehele, Morwellham, Halton Quay are only some of the places featured on this fascinating journey. At the end Sarah reflects that 'through the Tamar and its people I have found a new dimension'.

Sarah Foot

The River Tamar

MOST people first see the Tamar River as they cross the impressive toll bridge that leads from Devon to Cornwall via Plymouth to Saltash. Others glimpse it leaning out of the window of their Penzance bound train as it slowly rumbles across the magical and historical Brunel rail bridge.

As they look down from that lofty entrance to Cornwall and see the wide expanse of water, which is the estuary of the Tamar, littered with sailing boats and warships, tugs and fishing boats, they must wonder from whence this river comes.

For nearly ten years I was lucky enough to live within sight of the upper reaches of that river. From my bedroom window I could wake and see the curling snake of water as it wended its way past Halton Quay and then broadened towards those last tidal reaches at Weir Quay.

It was fascinating to watch the river in its many moods and I became intrigued with the complex history associated with it. To know more I went to find the beginning and end and the many points in between of a river that is unique in its dual role of being the boundary between Devon and Cornwall – and also the link.

Some 47 miles up stream from the Saltash bridge the story begins; and it was to this source that I went one day with a friend.

High up on unpicturesque and boggy scrubland, one overcast grey day, we squelched in among the marsh searching for the ever-lasting spring that would show us this was the river's birthplace. It was hard to tell, in the end, whether we found the actual spot. But there it seemed to be, seeping through the thick mud, and as we

The silvery ribbon of the Tamar makes its way majestically down to the sea.

6

followed the tiny rivulets we stopped to listen and heard the first song of the river. The sound, so pure and gentle, made us stand stock still and listen with a sort of reverence. With mud up to our knees and torn hands and sweaters from the brambles we had fought through, we felt more than recompensed for our trouble. The first soft sound of the recurring birth of the river was worth it all.

Only four miles north west of the source of the river lie the high cliffs of North Cornwall and Devon. Only these few miles keep Cornwall from becoming the island she sometimes seems to be. The Tamar, for most of its length, forms the boundary between Devon and Cornwall and is loved and respected by the people of both. I have often heard both Cornish people and Devonians describe their side of the river as 'the proper side'. As Rev John Prince, the Vicar of Berry Pomeroy, wrote in the nineteenth century, the Tamar 'amorously smiles on both counties'.

The name Tamar is said to mean 'Great Water' but there is a touching legend which describes how the river got its name.

It concerns a beautiful nymph called Tamara who was born in a cavern to parental spirits of the earth. To her parents' dismay she loved to roam in the upper world, enjoying the sunshine and the birdsong of which they disapproved. She would, at times, escape the cavern to swim in the streams and roam on the high land of Dartmoor. It was here that she met two young giants, Tavy and Tawrage, who followed her wherever she led them and completely lost their hearts to her.

They begged her to say which giant she preferred and to choose between them and put them out of their misery. For a while, like most young girls flattered by such attention, she led the two giants a merry dance all over the moor, darting away from them whenever they came too close.

When she finally consented to listen to their pleas more seriously her father found her, under a bush near Morwenstow, and in his fury he put the two giants into a deep sleep. When Tamara refused to return with him to the cavern he turned her into a spring that bubbled from the marshy meadow near Morwenstow, then seeped through

Slowly gathering force, the Tamar rushes through the arches of Greystone Bridge.

8

boggy land to become a stream and finally that flowing majestic River Tamar, making her permanent way down to the sea.

When the giants awoke from their deep sleep they returned to their home where they were also turned into streams. The Tavy was the lucky giant for he was to flow forever into the Tamar whereas the Tawridge became the Taw and flowed aimlessly in search of the Tamar but in the wrong direction. They say the Taw still mourns as he glides searching for his long lost love.

When Ptolemy wrote his Geography some 120 years after the birth of Christ, he found that there were three principal rivers in the country of the Dumnonian people: the Iska or Exe, the Tamare and the Kenion – perhaps the Fal. In 823 the Cornish were defeated by the Saxon Devonians at Gafulford, probably Caulford on the Lew in Devon, and it may have been as a result of this victory that Saxon settlers crossed the Tamar and colonized the vale of Attery. In the tenth century the Tamar was largely adopted for a boundary although the Attery settlements were awarded to Devon. This land fell into the hands of the Abbot of Tavistock and it was he who made sure that the land remained the property of Devon. However, recently, among a certain amount of confusion and disagreement, this land on the banks of the Attery or Ottery river has once again become Cornish.

The early childhood of the Tamar gives little intimation of the majesty of the later life of this grand river. For soon it wends its way under ancient bridges, through lush agricultural land, beneath low-hanging wooded areas, high cliffs and wide sweeping water meadows. It passes the now derelict mining areas where more copper, tin and silver were mined in the 1800s than anywhere else in Europe. Finally the Tamar meets the sea drifting under the bridges of Saltash, both old and modern, losing itself at last in that great sanctuary for shipping, Plymouth Sound.

A sleek and still youthful river flows steadily, ever on its way downward.

Tamar Lakes, Bude Canal, North Tamerton and Boyton

AT the source of the River Tamar at Woolly Barrows the country is shielded from the hard winds of the sea on the north coast. The little river takes its time to gain strength in hilly land wending its way towards the Tamar lakes.

The main Tamar lake is a huge man-made accomplishment. The great cement wall damming the water forces the river over its side in a daunting waterfall. From here to Launceston the river's life is inextricably linked with the old Bude Canal, for the smaller Tamar lake once fed the canal. Now it is a bird sanctuary and a well stocked coarse fishery, whereas the greater lake not only offers a water supply but amenities for fishing and sailing. The newly popular sport of surf sailing is also practised here with great enthusiasm.

The canal was built for the purpose of conveying sea sand from Bude to use as fertiliser on the inland farms which were of rather poor quality. It was first routed in 1774 and finally opened in 1823. In later years the canal carried larger quantities of other goods. Following the river from the lakes down to the parish of Werrington just to the north of Launceston, you will find continuous relics of parts of the canal still holding water. The river wends capriciously through this part of the valley, making its way in sudden curves and sharp bends under little hump-backed bridges and beside old mill houses. But the banks are largely overgrown and it is not easy to follow the river by foot.

In the days when the canal was being dug large snake nests were disturbed and the surrounding country was infested with snakes so that those working along the canal had to be wary of putting on their boots for fear of finding one nestling inside. The canal was closed in 1891 and so walking along the banks I felt sure the snakes had settled

Mirror-like reflections shimmer in the still surface of Tamar Lake when it was captured by Cornish photographer Ray Bishop in 1972.

back into tranquility.

Following the river southwards, I found on the west side two lovely churches set on hills overlooking the Tamar valley – North Tamerton and Boyton. I stopped and walked around the churchyards and looked at the magnificent views.

At Boyton I met two ladies busily decorating the church with a wonderful profusion of flowers, though they both said they wished I had come the week before to see the display they had made for Harvest Festival. Miss Vera Allin was born at Boyton and her father had once been the warden of the church. 'He loved the church', she told me. 'He came here to do things whenever he had any free time.'

She and her friend, Mrs Elizabeth Cowling, feel it their duty to give the church a 'lived-in' feeling, though congregations are sadly depleted. Once Boyton was a thriving little town with two general stores, three tailors, a carpenter, forge, petrol filling station, 'cycle repair shop and an old pound house where the farmers brought their

13

apples from miles around to make cider. Now little of this remains and Boyton is a quiet village housing those who have retired or find their work in nearby towns such as Launceston.

However, Boyton has provided homes and shelter since the very earliest days. On the eastern side of the river there was once an Iron Age fort or camp and just to the west of Bradridge Woods tumuli have been found.

There is evidence that a church has existed at Boyton since the thirteenth century, though it was enlarged in the fifteenth. The south aisle, where Mrs Cowling showed me some of the old surviving woodwork in the roof, is fifteenth century. It is interesting to note that in 1870 the Vicar of Boyton's daughter married the Marquess of Queensberry. His connection remains for in 1950 the Marquess of Queensberry unveiled the plaque to the war memorial. The early Norman font is made of Tintagel greenstone, a wonderfully irregular oval shape set on an hour-glass base. Altogether the church has a light, airy and welcoming atmosphere, and the view from the church-yard across dense woods and down to the Tamar is quite lovely. At the riverside is the old mill house, now renovated and used as a private house. It was still listed as a water mill in 1939.

In the 1600s, when this land by the river belonged to the Duchy of Cornwall, there seems to have been a bit of a mutiny amongst the tenants. They unlawfully felled and sold timber and built a mill on the Tamar thereby decreasing the effectiveness of the mill at Boyton. People were apparently taking what fish they wanted from the river and they illegally constructed a weir stopping the access of salmon and other fish. History does not relate how or if they were punished.

Werrington

ONE of the prettiest and most interesting parishes on the early banks of the Tamar is Werrington. It was here that the boundary line was fought over for so many years. The River Ottery or Attery meets the Tamar at this juncture. There seems to be a certain amount of disagreement among the local inhabitants about the name of this tributary of the Tamar. Miss Joan Rendell, a local historian, assures me the name is Attery and has been wrongly known as Ottery in recent years. In the 1600s Leland referred to the river as the Attery. When the bridge crossing the river at Yeolmbridge had a sign put on it marking the Ottery River she and other inhabitants complained and still hope to persuade the authorities to change the sign to Attery.

The great house of the district is Werrington Park now owned by the Williams family. Mr and Mrs Rob Williams invited me to lunch and showed me around the house and part of the estate.

The house has a magnificent situation overlooking the vale of Attery and a most varied history. The back wing, which is built around a courtyard, is the earliest part of the building and was once the property of that large landowner, the Abbot of Tavistock. At the Dissolution, King Henry VIII granted it to Lord John Russell. In the sixteenth century it was purchased by Sir Francis Drake, nephew of the great seaman and there is a stone above the door of the oldest part of the building dated 1641. During the Civil War this Sir Francis supported the Parliamentarians and his estate was given by Charles I to Sir Richard Grenville. However, during the Commonwealth the property was restored to the Drakes and in 1651 sold to Sir William Morice.

So that he could extend his bowling green, Sir William Morice removed the church, originally built next to the house, some distance away to where it stands now at the end of one of the great driveways to the house. The church was treated with the greatest disrespect, much of the stone being used for building and hedging. Graves were dug up and moved by cart, the bones being buried haphazardly, and the gravestones were, in some cases, used as paving stones.

The parishioners were so outraged at this behaviour that, it is said, they put a curse on the Morice family to make sure they would have no heirs. Sir William did, in fact, die childless and within thirty years all the estates of the Morice family had passed into strangers' hands. The new church was reconsecrated in 1743. In the late 1800s the Morice vault in the church was opened, and the remains of Sir William dressed complete in armour were found but left undisturbed where he remains there to this day.

Churches and churchyards tell so much of the history of the surrounding countryside. I often wonder how in the future people will be able to follow the history of country communities which in the past seem to have been kept forever in church records and amongst the relics and in the graveyards. For no longer is the church such a centre of the community.

Werrington church graveyard has a treasure trove of stories to tell. Fastened to the outside east wall of the church is the most heart-rending slate memorial depicting Sir Francis, his wife and four children all kneeling. Drake has his sorrowing face turned to view those who view him.

But probably the most moving memorial I have ever seen in any churchyard is now attached to the north wall of the church. It was being used as a paving stone and was rescued and fixed to the wall for safety. It reads:

Deposited Here
Are the Remains of Philip Scipio
Servant to the Duke of Wharton
An African
Whose Quality Might Have done Honour
To any Nation or Climate
And Gives us to See
That Virtue is Confined
To No Country or Complexion
Here Weep
Uncorrupted Fidelity
And Plain Honesty

Werrington Park, home of Mr and Mrs Rob Williams, has a magnificent setting overlooking the vale of Attery.

In a Pious Regard to which Virtue
Approved by a Brother and Husband.
The Rt. Hon. Lady Lucy Morice. 10th September 1734.

This is one of only six such stones in the whole of Great Britain erected to the memory of slaves by their 'owners'. Scipio was brought to Werrington by the renegade Duke of Wharton, who left Werrington in a hurry leaving his slave behind who was then 'adopted' by Lady Lucy Morice.

In this graveyard, too, is the stone marking the grave of five children of one family who were all victims of the cholera epidemic of 1842 which raged in Devon and Cornwall. All five children of one family died within one week.

There is one last piece of local history to relate in this remarkable churchyard: the gravestone of Noah Smale. It marks the resting place of a man who followed an occupation which no longer exists. He was the last plane keeper of the Bude Canal which closed in 1891. His job

17

was to supervise the tug-boats which were hauled up and down the incline plane on the canal as it ran through the parish and he was responsible for patrolling and keeping in good order his section of the canal.

On the day I visited Werrington Park, Mr and Mrs Williams welcomed me most warmly and I could well believe the story they told me about the gentlemen who were redrawing the county boundary. They came to lunch at Werrington where they were so well entertained that they lost their way afterwards and drew the boundary along the banks of the Attery instead of the Tamar. Now that the Tamar is finally the boundary in this area I asked Mr Williams whether it made any difference to him. 'Yes' he said, 'I think I prefer to be Cornish although I don't know why it should matter'. The Williams are, after all, one of the oldest Cornish families. Mr Rob Williams' brother Julian, lives at another famous Cornish house, Caerhays Castle.

After lunch Mrs Williams took me to see the older part of the house, recently wrecked by fire, which they are slowly restoring. Her father-in-law had become dispirited about living in the big house after the fearful fire. People sleeping in that part of the house had a narrow escape. The damage of such a fire is appalling. Huge great beams blackened and pitted but still standing, the staircase and ceiling ruined, windows blown out by the heat.

Mr Williams then took me for a drive through the beautiful parkland curving gently down to the river. The great drive planted with lime trees is a magnificent sight. We went to look at Druxton Wharf, once the farthest place the tub-boats had come along the Bude Canal. Now it is just an empty basin in the land. How strange it must have been to see boats meandering through the fields. Druxton Bridge is low and pretty and if you stand on the banks of the river you get a marvellous view through the rounded arches.

Werrington is a lovely part of the countryside quite unlike any other part of Cornwall, with a magic of its own. So many varied people have lived and worked and followed their ambitions here. Yet now it seems secluded from the world, quite untouched by modern times.

Just above Netherbridge the Ottery or Attery joins the Tamar. This is a fourteenth century bridge with an old milestone in the middle telling us we are two miles from Launceston.

Launceston

LAUNCESTON is the gateway to Cornwall. This lovely medieval town, once the only walled town in Cornwall, still gives the impression of being set within fortifications, although most of the old walls are now demolished. The North Gate of these walls was demolished in 1834 and the line of the walls can still be seen in the curve of the houses. But South Gate still stands and it is always a thrill to drive through the old stone gateway and to enter the town. Once there was a tree that grew from these stalwart walls and many of the old prints show the tree still incomprehensibly thriving there. More recently the tree was taken away as it was felt the roots would eventually demolish the old stonework.

Until 1835 Launceston was the county town of Cornwall, it then yielded that honour to Bodmin and now Truro vies for it. It remains an agricultural town and as John Betjeman wrote in his *Shell Guide* 'For this reason there are eighteenth century houses worthy of a county town. The most solid of these are the eighteenth century mansions on either side of Castle Street. They are built of what was then a precious rarity in Cornwall, red brick. This little street, which was cobbled until 1956, is the most perfect collection of eighteenth century town houses in Cornwall. The fertile gardens slope sharply down and the house windows look across to the steep hills opposite. Their street fronts are protected by ironwork gates and low walls.'

The castle sits in its majesty above the town and yet close to the buildings huddled around it. If you have a head for heights the view from the keep of this old castle is one of the most staggering vistas in Cornwall. You can see right across to Dartmoor on the one hand and the lovely peaks of Bodmin Moor – Brown Willy and Rough Tor – stand out against the sky line on the other. In between lies the gentle valley of the Tamar and her estuaries.

The castle is still known by its Norman name, Dunheved Castle,

Granite built St Mary Magdalene Church is the only one of its kind in Cornwall.

though it is thought there was a castle here before the Normans came. But much of the masonry structure belongs to the first half of the thirteenth century and is probably due to Richard, Earl of Cornwall. Eventually Edward III bestowed it on the Black Prince, the first Duke of Cornwall, and since then the sequence of inheritance by the heirs to the British crown has survived to this day.

In 1909 King George V, and in 1921 the Duke of Windsor, visited the castle in their capacity as Dukes of Cornwall. And in 1937 King George VI, already crowned, made a state entry to the castle and was presented with the feudal dues, a pound of pepper and one hundred shillings, which were set down in a charter of 1230 by Richard, King of the Romans, Earl of Cornwall. More recently, in 1973, Prince Charles

Launceston's South Gate.

also visited the castle to receive his feudal dues.

The church of St Mary Magdelene is the only one of its kind in Cornwall. Built of granite it is intricately carved in a most amazing way, for granite is a hard and difficult stone to work on. The story is that in 1511 Sir Henry Trecarrel was in the middle of making an addition to his house to the south of Launceston when his only son, still a baby, died by drowning in the bath. He immediately stopped work on the house and rebuilt the church instead, as a sort of memorial to his dead baby.

Once I was walking through the town on a Sunday afternoon and heard someone practising the organ in the church. The music swelled around the narrow, quiet streets and seemed to fill the whole town. So in a way it is nice that this magnificent church is among the buildings on the hilly slopes, but it does mean that one can never have an unbroken view of the great monument to a man's grief at the loss of his baby son.

Charles Causley, the world famous poet, was born in Launceston and has lived here most of his life except for a short time in the Navy. He has written a poem about the building of the church:

For twelve years and one in Launceston town
The masons wore fifty flint fingers down
Carving an angel, a rose and a clown
On every inch of the Magdelene's crown.

Charles Causley has fought shy of becoming a professional Cornishman. He loves to travel and does so, reading his poetry all over the world from Paris to Israel, the United States and Australia. But Cornish people count him very much as one of their own and particularly in his home town.

I met him for lunch one day in the White Hart Inn in the square of Launceston where once the market used to be held. He was welcomed by almost everyone who could catch his eye and reminded by some of a childhood escapade or a poetry reading.

With his peaked hat and his walking stick he is a distinctive figure in Launceston. What was it like to be famous? I asked him. A slight twinkle came to his eye and he answered, 'None of this is real'.

As a boy he turned his sights to the wider world beyond his own country, looking outwards rather than down to the darker depths of Cornwall. A journey to north or west Cornwall was always

Charles Causley the world famous poet.

considered a dangerous adventure.

An only child with a father who died when he was a youngster, he was turned in on himself a great deal and already wrote plays and novels in his teens. Then the war came and he went off into the Navy and still kept writing those poems in his head. He already had the confidence to know that one day he would write for a living.

But first he was to be a schoolmaster in the school in his home town where once he had been a pupil. He contributed to the local community and looked after his mother, who, for several years, needed a great deal of care. 'I could never have kept her at home without plenty of help from my friends, and it was made easier being in a town where I knew everyone', he told me.

As a young man he loved to listen to poets read their own work and remembers hearing Lous MacNeice, Auden, Day Lewis and Graves while he profoundly regrets never meeting that other great

Cornish writer Sir Arthur Quiller Couch.

He has also befriended most of today's poets and travelled with them on unforgettable poetry reading trips. Just as he praises their poetry they have returned the compliment. It was only in 1987 when a very special volume of tributes from his fellow poets was published by the Cornish publishers, Peterloo Poets to celebrate Causley's 70th birthday that I realized how much he is admired by his fellow scribes.

The impressive volume contains poems dedicated to Charles Causley by many of his friends including Ted Hughes, Roger McGough, Philip Larkin and John Heath Stubbs with some prose tributes from such writers as D. M. Thomas, Colin MacInnes and J. C. Trewin.

There are many throughout the nation and, I suspect, most of the long term residents of Launceston, who think that Charles Causley should have been Poet Laureate after John Betjeman, but it matters little about official titles. The important thing is Charles Causley is a genuine man who has written, and is still writing, very fine poetry. Because sometimes he has written specifically for children, in many cases his poems are a child's first introduction to the world of poetry. How lucky they are to have such an introduction, and how lucky we in Cornwall are to have such a poet to whom we can so easily relate. Cornish people have always had a keen sense of appreciation of their own, and they have not overlooked the fact that Charles Causley is a fellow citizen of whom to be proud.

Looking downstream from Polson Bridge, once the main entrance to Cornwall from Devon.

Lifton and The Lyd

THE Lyd, one of the prettiest tributaries of the Tamar, runs beside the little town of Lifton and it was there I went to meet Anne Voss-Bark one of the best known and best loved inhabitants of this area. She came to Lifton nearly 30 years ago to run the fishing inn, the Arundell Arms, and has turned it into one of Britain's most famous fishing retreats.

This elegant and attractive woman, so ultra-feminine, was once an actress and later highly successful in the advertising world. When her first husband became seriously ill with bronchitis and they were advised to move out of London, they decided to try and run a hotel of this sort. She did a crash course at a friend's hotel in London and then started at the deep end, learning as she went. It must be due to her strong nature, extreme efficiency and real charm that the inn has such an atmosphere of friendly, quiet warmth. People return year after year and now more visitors arrive from abroad especially from Holland.

When her first husband died she decided to continue running the hotel and later she married Mr Conrad Voss-Bark, once a BBC parliamentary correspondent, whom she met when he came to stay at the hotel. They live in a house they built overlooking the Lyd.

The terrific increase in the interest in fishing she puts down to the fact that so many people now are overworked and living under great pressure and they find fishing the most relaxing and enjoyable way of getting away from it all. And she too has found it a wonderful way of relaxing. If she feels worn out or fed up she tells everyone she'll be unavailable for a few hours and with rod in hand she wanders off down the river bank. She finds this quiet sport in picturesque surroundings wonderful therapy. The hotel has twenty miles of fishing on the Tamar and the Lyd.

Mrs Voss-Bark is also an enthusiastic preserver of things past. She

Mrs Ann Voss-Bark outside Lifton's former cockpit which is now the fishing tackle room at the Arundell Arms.

showed me the outbuildings of the hotel, once the main complex of the village. You can see where the old court room once was, the cells still complete with bars, the little flat for the local policeman and the police station. In the basement of what was the old schoolhouse she has made a marvellous skittle alley. In the terraced garden she has restored the old cockpit where once the horrible blood-thirsty cock fights were cheered and jeered. It now makes a perfect home for all the fishing tackle of the visitors to the hotel.

One bright, sunny, autumn day I walked along the river with Roy Buckingham, now the fishing instructor at the Arundell Arms. He has worked on this part of the Lyd and the Tamar for twenty years first as

The Arundell Arms, Lifton.

a water bailiff and now as an instructor. He knows every pool, rock and sandy cove like the back of his hand. He loves the river and its banks.

We walked down the Lyd towards Lydfoot, where it joins the Tamar. 'Would you like to see the heronry?' he asked me. Across the field we went to look in amazement at the mass of huge straggly nests, now deserted, of those great majestic river birds. The bird life of this river is most varied. We saw a green woodpecker flit across our path, dazzlingly bright, flaunting his beauty as if he knew how impressed we would be. Then a fat jay flew from the trees towards the river. The black ominous cormorants are the birds these fishermen and protectors of the river hate to see for they will dive for fish so greedily and do more damage to the stock of fish then any other bird.

On the banks of the Lyd we came across the ruins of an old

28

railway bridge, only the two outside stalwarts left. Once this bit of the railway went from Launceston to Tavistock via Lydford, following the Lyd. What a marvellous railway journey that must have been.

Roy Buckingham considers himself lucky to have spent twenty years on the river. He has that elusive quality of life – job satisfaction. Sometimes he is on the river all day and most of the night as a lot of the visitors at the hotel enjoy night fishing. He was born, and has always lived, at Launceston and loves the area. From boyhood he enjoyed fishing and has competed and won many of the casting competitions all over the country.

Down by the river we watched as a herd of cows came to drink their fill and cool their hooves in the water after their sun baking of that bright morning. I asked Roy if this upset the fish when he was fishing, but he told me that it does more good than harm. The cows disturb minute bits of weed and the insects among them when they come to paddle. If you go further downstream you will often see the trout coming up to feed on these small bits of nourishment.

In the winter Roy busies himself with tying flies, which he does for the shop at the hotel as well as for himself, and with making sure that all the banks and steps down to the pools are in good order and properly cleared. Although the river is stocked with fish from the hatcheries, he says you can always tell if you are playing a wild fish. They are cleverer and more difficult to catch and know best where to hide themselves in the shadows away from fishermen. Like all huntsmen he respects his quarry.

I was reminded that day how easy it is to fall in love with a river. Can there be anything to compare with the dappled light that falls on deep, clear, bright water on a sunny still day? Or the cows taking deep draughts of fresh water, the birds darting with flashes of light beneath the trees, the wide meadows so rich from the irrigation the river affords them? That birth song we heard high up at Woolley Barrows was still being repeated, but with stronger more varied tones from this growing river.

I went with Roy Buckingham to visit Polson Bridge, once the main entrance to Cornwall from Devon. But now there is a new bridge built over the bypass called Dunheved Bridge. I like the feudal story of Polson Bridge. Apparently certain lands in Cardinham were held by the service of meeting the Earl at his entry into Cornwall by the bridge and bearing his riding cloak for forty days or 'as long as he should tarry in his county'.

29

Greystone Bridge and Endsleigh

FROM Lydfoot the river winds through pretty country until it comes to a steep wooded valley where the road from Launceston to Tavistock crosses at old Greystone Bridge. Charles Henderson called it 'the fairest bridge in the two Shires which it links together . . . for beauty of situation and perfection of form Greystone Bridge has no superior in the two Western Counties.'

Both Greystone and Horsebridge – further down the river – are, I think, equally as beautiful. They were indulgence bridges which perhaps accounts for their almost holy atmosphere. To encourage people to help, both financially and practically, to build bridges and keep them in good repair, the Church offered indulgences usually on forty days. Prayers would be said for those who helped to build the bridge and it was believed that they would receive some pardon in later life for their earthly sins.

It seems a wicked way to get people to help build bridges but somehow the faith in which it was done lingers among the great grey stones that make up the strong arches that now carry modern traffic without any detriment to the bridge. These bridges were built long before even carriages were in common use and the passes down to them were once treacherously steep and narrow. Only pack mules came with goods they transported all over the country.

One soft day in late summer when the mists around the valley slowly lifted and the sun came gently through, I walked along the banks of the Tamar with Grace Norman from Greystone Bridge to Endsleigh, once the holiday home of the Duke of Bedford. Grace Norman was brought up next door to Endsleigh at Leigh Barton Farm where her family had been farmers for over 400 years.

For the pure joy of enjoying truly grand, yet secluded, peaceful river scenery I don't think there is a more wonderful walk along the

Greystone Bridge 'the fairest bridge in the two shires which it links together.'

Tamar than those miles from Greystone Bridge down to Horsebridge, and then beyond to Gunnislake. It is private property. We had been given permission and had to be careful not to disturb the fishermen we met on the way silently concentrating on their sport.

As we walked Grace Norman reminisced about her riverside childhood. 'My father used to make up fairy stories to tell us about the dragon of Cornwall. We always thought of Cornwall as the dangerous side of the river and sometimes when we were swimming there we would play games daring each other to swim across and land on the Cornish bank. It was a very brave thing to do in our eyes.' It is true there is a sharp difference between the banks of Devon and Cornwall along this walk. The Cornish side from the water rises far more steeply and gives the impression of being more dangerous and forbidding whereas the Devon banks consist of wide lush water meadows gently leading down to the dark pools of the Tamar.

High above us loomed the great Bishop's Rock where it is said a bishop could preach and the congregation down on the banks could

Endsleigh House looks as if it were designed for fun rather than beauty or practicality.

hear his every word, the acoustics were so good. Next to Bishop's Rock are the daunting cliffs of Cartha Martha, so grey and steep and sheer they blotted out the sky above.

As we neared Endsleigh House, now a hotel, we saw more signs of civilisation. Here are the wide rides laid by the Duke of Bedford which were swept clean of leaves when he travelled along them. Grace Norman can remember well the days when the grandfather of the present Duke would come with his huge entourage of staff to stay at Endsleigh. His wife, the 'flying Duchess', would often come in her little aeroplane and land on the fields above the house. As we climbed up the hill towards this unusual, most wonderfully situated house, she pointed out to me the little swimming pool built for the Duchess among the rhododendrons and bamboos so that she could swim in complete privacy.

It is hard to describe the magic of Endsleigh. Built during the Regency by the 6th Duke of Bedford for his wife Georgiana in the style of a 'cottage orné' it was designed by Jeffry Wyatville while the landscape gardens were the responsibility of Humphry Repton.

The house looks as if it were designed for fun rather than beauty or practicality and has undulating, irregular, grey roofs and little ornate verandahs and patios. But the real wonder of the place is to stand at the front of the house and look down across the sweeping lawns past the plantations of great and rare trees and rhododendrons to the wide sweeping river.

Grace Norman told me that the Duke of Bedford had so disliked the sound of motor mowers that the lawns were always cut by men with scythes all working in unison and the pattern they formed on the grass was truly wonderful to see.

In the huge grounds there are many follies and little cottages. We went to visit the pond cottage and there is a little stone building of a holy well originally built at Leigh Barton by the Abbot of Tavistock, who had once owned all the land about. Grace's mother, Mrs Blanchard, told me she thought it a most strange thing that the Bedfords had moved the well to Endsleigh. 'After all, the water can no longer be holy now that they have moved it from the original spring', she said.

There was a tragedy when the late Duke of Bedford was found dead in the woods after a shooting accident. Since then the house has not been used by the Russell family. More recently it was sold to a syndicate who run it as a hotel, largely connected with the salmon fishing.

Horace Adams is in semi-retirement now but he has worked on the Endsleigh estate since he left school and his father worked there before him. For years now he has been the guardian of this stretch of the river and has become one of the best loved characters of the area. He has fished with three generations of the Russell family and known many of the famous people who have come to fish this part of the Tamar. One day he and I walked along the river from Endsleigh towards Horsebridge. He told me how happy his life had been and it is clear from his stories that it was not only the river he loved but the people he had met and talked to.

He has been known to have particular success in teaching women to fish and thinks they often have more potential in this sport because they have greater patience. But it is not only his fishing knowledge that those who come to Endsleigh seek out, it is his congenial company. He told me that he often enjoys more than one lunchtime picnic by the river in the season as everyone insists he joins them.

As we walked along the river I could see each pool recalling some great experience for him. He can remember his father helping in the building of the great stone croys; quite a feat digging in and planting the huge granite blocks that form the deep pools above and the rushing water below. They were firmly built and no torrential rains or rushing water have dislodged them. Horace Adams has seen many changes at Endsleigh but he is like the great stone croys, indestructible and forever part of the river.

We walked through the thickly wooded area along the wide water meadows; we watched a huge heron fly up river touching the water with his wide wings; we heard, every now and then, the comforting plop of a rising fish, and all the time Horace Adams regaled me with stories so that his voice and the sound of the river merged into one.

It is fortunate that Horace Adams' successor loves the River Tamar just as well.

I have been with him along the water meadow drives that he walks almost daily on his beat from Horrabridge to Greystone Bridge. At 28, Bob Wellard had been the river-keeper here for four years and already had an intimate knowledge of this stretch of river.

He was a commando in the army previously and although he was brought up in the city of Birmingham he had always been drawn to countryside pursuits and particularly to rivers. He started fishing as a young boy and it has been in his blood ever since.

His job, which he enjoys to the full, is multi-faceted. He must keep the river clear of fallen trees and branches, he must know where the herons, cormorants and otters are likely to filch his fish. But more seriously he must also be aware of where the poachers are likely to strike. Poaching for the pot is a thing of the past, and when it does exist is not a greatly worrying factor for the river keepers of today.

But big business poaching is becoming more and more prevalent with each passing year. Bob Wellard assures me that as many fish that are caught legally in the Tamar river are also netted illegally, with some poachers making hundreds of pounds. They are now highly organised into criminal groups.

It is his duty to work alongside the river bailiffs employed by the water authority to make sure that as few fish as possible disappear from his river illegally through the season. He has had to apprehend poachers in the middle of the night on occasions, and admits that it can be quite frightening, but finds that if he is firm and unrelenting poachers caught in the act will usually not argue with him.

34

A handsome three-pound Sea Trout taken from the river near Endsleigh.

Protecting his stretch of the river is something that he does instinctively and with great care. He says that no-one would be a river keeper for the money, and that you have to be interested in wild life and enjoy being part of the river to make the most of the job.

Not long before I met him he had been returning from the river one evening in the dark when he heard a loud rumbling noise. Standing still he peered into the murky night wondering what intruders would appear. Then he saw them, a herd of red deer, charging down the hill and then splashing through the shallow waters to cross the river. Remembering the sight and sound of this strange apparition still moves him.

'Sometimes when the visitors at the hotel have gone to dinner at about half past seven, I'll take my rod and fish on my own. Then I know why I am a river keeper,' he said as he watched the waters tumbling over the black rock below the hotel.

Now that both the Swiss Cottage and the Pond Cottage in the

A fisherman tests his skill.

grounds have been restored by the Landmark Trust and are rented out throughout the year, there are more and more people coming to enjoy the beauties of the Endsleigh Estate. With shooting parties in the winter run by the owner of much of the land hereabouts – Mr Philip Tuckett – and with the fishing facilities offered from March until October, Endsleigh is a place of beauty with much else besides.

The farmhouses that are built right down on the water's edge on both the Devon and the Cornish banks are of stoic beauty. No bijou residences here, these houses are built to last against all weathers. Like the river, which views they all enjoy, these houses have an enduring quality about them.

Most of the fishing takes place from the Devon banks and now that Bob Wellard will also be running tuition classes in fishing there will be an ever growing attraction to visiting this part of the Tamar River.

Close to the hotel and in the impressive grounds of Endsleigh is a thriving Garden Centre to which people travel from many miles to buy rare and strong plants.

Leigh Barton and
The Swiss Cottage

LEIGH Farm is the next building on the river after Endsleigh.
Mrs Blanchard and her daughter, Grace Norman, now live at Milton
Abbot, but it was they who told me so many stories about the house
and their 400 year connection with it.

'There is a ghost there', Mrs Blanchard said, 'but he is quite
friendly and I never minded being left alone in the house.' The ghost
is thought to be that of a monk and is said to be heard walking just
before the death of the man of the house.

The earliest record of a dwelling at Leigh is in the year 927.
It belonged to Tavistock Abbey until its dissolution when King
Henry VIII gave it to 'those interlopers the Russells'. The 400 year
connection of the Blanchard family from those days until a few years
ago as tenant farmers must be almost unique. But even before the
Blanchard family's connection Mrs Mary Blanchard told me her own
family the Wards had lived there.

Mrs Blanchard is in her nineties now and though happily settled
in Milton Abbot she talks most lovingly about Leigh Barton. She told
me that they had always kept up the old custom on Christmas Eve of
burning Greenash, cut and faggoted, in the huge granite fireplace in
the kitchen. The custom is supposed to have derived from the night
when Jesus was born and Joseph had gone out and cut the Greenash
to light a fire to warm the new-born baby and his mother. Also in the
great kitchen, she told me, they had unforgettable Harvest Suppers –
anything between 30 and 40 people sitting at the huge kitchen table.

The present owner of Leigh Farm is Philip Tuckett. His father
bought the land from the Russells in the 1950s and he inherited it
when his father died. When he took me to see the house he was still
unmarried and not living at Leigh Barton. He and his mother invited

me to see the house and I was intrigued to go having heard so much about it from its former occupiers.

The kitchen was exactly as I had imagined it from Mrs Blanchard's description. And although the house has been added to and renovated and some of the older parts removed – the Bedfords apparently took the old staircase and the mullion windows out for use elsewhere – there is still a feeling of timelessness there. Out on the small terraced garden I could easily imagine hooded monks walking, arms folded saying their vespers.

Probably the most staggering part of the house are the great arches of the roof beams. It was well worth climbing through the small entrance in a bedroom ceiling to see this sight and marvel that they should have lasted so long with the wooden rivets, a masterpiece of carpentry reminiscent of an old barge turned upside down.

At one time there was no upstairs to this house and in the great rooms downstairs you could look up at this glorious arched woodwork, once the ceiling to the whole building. Draughty it must have been but it seems a great shame that these beautiful trusses are now hidden from view.

There is a beautiful great barn alongside the house and a round house with the old pillar and shafts once turned by a pony and used for grinding corn. Grace Norman told me that in her childhood they had used it as a roundabout turning the shafts quickly and jumping on them for a ride.

The friendly atmosphere of the house extends to the gardens and the outbuildings. 'It was always a very comforting house,' Grace Norman told me. 'Whenever you came into it, it seemed to fold itself around you and if you were miserable it seemed to say, 'poor thing, never mind'. In 1981 Philip Tuckett was married to Antonia Darwell and went to live at Leigh Barton which has been his home ever since.

Having seen Leigh Barton, Philip Tuckett drove me to visit the Swiss Cottage which was built in the early 1800s by the Duke of Bedford on the Endsleigh estate so that his wife and daughters could go to this romantic spot and have picnics in complete comfort.

The strange little house all thatched and wooden with ornate carvings on its windowsills and a verandah on the second floor with one of the most astounding views I have ever seen, was bought by the Tucketts and then sold to the Landmark Trust which has restored the cottage with great care.

If you stand on the verandah on a sunny morning you can watch

Swiss Cottage, built in the early 1800s by the Duke of Bedford on the Endsleigh estate so that his wife and daughters could picnic in comfort.

the river hundreds of feet below; the land falls from the cottage very steeply and is thickly clothed in huge and wonderful trees. There, threading its way through the forest, is the silver jewel of a river. And all around is quiet and still except for the whispering of the trees and the odd call of a pheasant. I could imagine how exciting it must have been for children to walk through the woods from Endsleigh and visit this secret place.

Cartha Martha

ON the Cornish banks of the Tamar just up river from Endsleigh I had seen the great cliffs of Cartha Martha and through the trees had managed to just pick out a house up there.

Discovering that Dr and Mrs Jonas lived there I got their permission to visit them and see the view from that wonderful position. And wonderful it certainly is and almost perilous as well. The precipice of rock seems to arch over the river and on the arch with the river nearly hidden underneath sits the little house.

Originally this too was all Bedford land. The house that was once here was used as a guest house although the Duke had once had a large aviary there as he had had one in the woods at Endsleigh for his remarkable collection of budgerigars.

However, when Dr and Mrs Jonas bought the land they had pulled down the old house. 'It was terribly haunted', Mrs Jonas told me, 'there had been two suicides here and the atmosphere was so terrible no one could possibly have lived in it.' When the builders had arrived to demolish the old house, they had asked Mrs Jonas why she was intent on pulling down the house. 'I told them that it was haunted but I don't think they really believed me until they went inside. Then they came right out and said they understood exactly what I meant.'

But Mrs Jonas believes that the instant the roof was taken off the bad spirits were released, for the ground that they have built their new house on is certainly not in any way haunted and the wooden bungalow has a very happy atmosphere. And what a wonderful view. Through the wooded valley all those hundreds of feet below you can see the river like a shining snake making its way towards Endsleigh and then you turn and watch its earlier journey as it comes down

Upstream from Endsleigh House.

from Greystone Bridge.

Suicides there may have been in this area but there is now a perfect sense of peace and calm, stronger than almost anywhere else that I walked. Mrs Jonas took me through the wooded walk where the beech trees filtered the late summer sunlight and we stood on Bishop's Rock and looked down at the great vista of the valley.

Just here, in a glade of wonderful old trees where there is a special sort of hush about the place, there are the old earth works of an Iron Age encampment. So this particular spot was chosen all those hundreds of years ago as a place to live. And rightly so for it is a remarkable situation looking across to the fields of the Devon banks on the other side of the river.

If you make your way down from this high spot to the river along the rides made by the Duke of Bedford you can walk along the banks to where the Inny joins the Tamar. The woodland all around belongs to the Earl of Bradford, who owns most of the woodland on the opposite bank as well.

Horsebridge and
The Horn of Plenty

HORSEBRIDGE, almost a twin to Greystone Bridge, was granted an Indulgence in 1437. There are curious brackets built of stone on the upstream side of this bridge believed to be connected with a salmon weir or stake net. This could indicate the lowest limit of the Abbot of Tavistock's fishery.

Like Greystone this bridge and the surroundings have a particularly peaceful atmosphere. The hamlet on the Devon banks fits snugly into the hillside and there is a pretty little inn with arched windows. The older parts of this building have been there since the Abbot of Tavistock's days.

From Horsebridge down to Gunnislake is another wonderful walk with the fields and wooded places ablaze with buttercups and campion in the summer. In a pool not far from Gunnislake my husband caught his first salmon helped by another water-keeper, Herbie Symons. He, like Horace Adams and Roy Buckingham, has spent most of his life on his beat of the river. What better praise can a fisherman have than the ultimate compliment from a fellow guardian of the water. That great fisherman Horace Adams, when speaking about Herbie Symons, said to me, 'He is the best fisherman I have ever known. If he says he's going to catch a fish you can be sure he will'.

Herbie Symons is now retired but he has walked and fished this part of the river for years and if you watch him walking along the banks you can see that his eyes are taking in movements and shadows in the water that only he has learned to see. It is almost as if he and the river can converse, the relationship is so close. Last year he went away from the Tamar for the first time in his life, to fish in Scotland.

Just above the river, before you reach Newbridge at Gunnislake, there is a house, once called Tamar View, but now renamed the Horn

42

Sonia Stevenson outside the restaurant she runs with husband Patrick.

of Plenty by its owners, Sonia and Patrick Stevenson. They have turned this house on the hill above the Tamar into one of the most famous small restaurants in the country and this is due to the magical art of Mrs Stevenson's cooking. She was the first woman to be invited to cook at Maxim's in Paris and has received almost every accolade a chef could possibly hope to have.

She and her husband were originally musicians living in London and the idea of cooking started as a sort of game. Patrick was always extremely fussy about his food and soon taught his young wife the kind of food a discerning gourmet liked. They ate every so often in good restaurants or with friends who were accomplished cooks and slowly by experimenting they started a whole galaxy of recipes of their own.

'We used to have a trial by asking about five groups of friends to turn up between seven and nine for dinner and doing the whole thing from start to finish as if we were running a restaurant. It was the best

Sonia Stevenson at work in her kitchen.

way to learn about getting things ready beforehand and how to cope if everyone arrived at the same time'. For some time they had been experimenting with one new dish each week so that when the restaurant opened in 1967 they were well in practice.

I am sure the reason for their ever-growing success is that cooking remains a sort of celebration for Sonia. By the way she handles the large slabs of meat and the unusual vegetables in her kitchen and in the way she describes the sauces she is about to concoct, it is blatantly obvious she enjoys it all and treats it still as a form of creativity. Patrick remains the perfectionist and judge. She is the one who obviously never worries, always feels things will work out for the best. Patrick keeps her exuberance and optimism in check.

44

The Horn of Plenty is the sort of place those who really love fine food will go for a treat; it is not the sort of place to go for a quick snack. Just as Sonia Stevenson finds the cooking a celebration so the eating should be done in the same vein.

But before this house was a restaurant it had known a very different form of life. For this was once the home of Moses Bawden, the mine engineer for the Devon Great Consols Mine which mined more copper than any other mine in the whole of Europe in the 1800s. So this house really marks the first sign of mining on my travels down the Tamar. From here on the sounds of the riverside had been very different to the quiet call of birds and gentle solitary song of the river. For once the overriding noise of this part of the valley was the turning waterwheels and the hefty sighs and groans they made as they used the water to perform so many tasks involved with mining.

The story goes that when the Devon Great Consols Mine was eventually closed in November 1901, Moses Bawden was ill in bed in his room upstairs at Tamar View. When the dreaded news was brought to him he turned his face to the wall and burst into tears.

The closure of the mine affected 351 employees. The Duke of Bedford guaranteed employment for most of them for the rest of the winter on his estates and to some who had been working over forty years he gave a pension. Since he had obtained £250,000 in royalties from the mines in which he had taken little or no interest, he could obviously well afford this gesture. Previously he had built 250 mining houses around Gulworthy, Tavistock and Morwellham in 1849 when the overcrowding in the area had become acute and the Portreeve of Tavistock had sponsored a petition for the release of land for houses. All the land from Tavistock to the Tamar had belonged to the Duke.

The seventh Duke of Bedford, after the closure of the mines, was anxious to restore his lands to their old state and no time was wasted in having the shafts filled and the surface buildings levelled. By 1907 there was little evidence to be seen on the Ordnance Survey map of what had once been the biggest copper mine in Europe.

After the closure of the mines Tamar View was used by the Duke of Bedford's agent and for several years this position was held by Mr T S Bliss who was apparently always known by his initials TSB. In 1980 I went to talk to his wife who was in her 90s – she has since died but at that time she lived at Sydenham Damerel. When her husband retired the Duke gave him the Mill Lodge and six acres of land where Mrs Bliss lived.

I went to find Mrs Bliss and she talked to me in her little upstairs sitting room. She did not remember much, her memory was failing her over dates, facts and figures, but she told me 'We had a gorgeous life, you couldn't call it anything else, the Duke was a fine man to work for. We used to go up to the Duke's estate in Scotland and that was how we met the Kaiser. He was quite an ordinary man and very nice to us.'

She, too remembered the 'flying Duchess' coming in to land in her aeroplane on the fields above Endsleigh and the tragic night when she set off from Woburn to accumulate more solo flying hours and was never seen again.

'My husband was a great fisherman and the Duke would often ask us to join him for a picnic by the river, then they would all go out on boats', Mrs Bliss told me. She remembered having as a pet a blackbird that her children had found with a broken wing. She used to walk along the lanes towards Endsleigh and the blackbird would sit on her shoulder. One day when out walking she met the Duchess. 'She said she would like to have a pet blackbird too, and when I next went over to Endsleigh I saw a blackbird tied up next to the gardener's house and they told me the Duchess had asked them to catch one and tame it. I told them that they would never tame a bird unless it wanted to be tamed, and I think they eventually let it go and told the Duchess it had escaped.'

She had many happy memories and kept repeating, 'We had such a happy life'.

Newbridge and Morwellham

NOT far from the Horn of Plenty, the lovely Newbridge at Gunnislake majestically straddles the River Tamar. I have loved this bridge at Gunnislake since my childhood when coming back to the family home at Callington for school holidays my grandfather would meet us at Tavistock station. Crossing the Tamar at Gunnislake we would spell out D-E-V-O-N and then C-O-R-N-W-A-L-L. On the last letter we would reach the Cornish bank with a great shout of joy. So to me crossing this bridge always meant coming home.

This bridge, Leland informs us in 1539, was built by Sir Piers Edgcumbe who was lord of the famous Tamarside mansion of Cotehele in the late 1400s and early 1500s. Later it was to see a lot of action during the Civil War. Sir Richard Grenville defended it against Lord Essex on July 20, 1644, but after a battle Essex took the bridge with the loss of about 40 men. The Royalists lost about 200, killed and taken prisoner. It is hard to think such bloody battles were fought in this quiet part of the valley. Almost impossible to imagine the banks and bridge strewn with dead and dying bodies.

Gunnislake retains the atmosphere more of an abandoned mining town than of a battlefield. There is something haunting about the place as if the suffering of the miners who worked under such terrible conditions has left its mark about the steep slopes and among the closely huddled houses.

From Newbridge the River Tamar is tidal and slowly starts to unfold the beauty of its great estuary. But here the cliffs are high especialy the magnificent grey crags of Morwell Rocks on the Devon bank which can be viewed from miles about on the Cornish side of the river.

Just below the bridge there is a weir and signs of the old manure canal dug when the river was the chief way of moving goods and

Newbridge at Gunnislake straddles the Tamar.

travelling. Until 1962 there was no road bridge across the Tamar below Gunnislake for the nineteen miles to the sea. Once barges of 300 tons could navigate the river to the port of Morwellham and 50 ton barges with coal and manure threaded their way as far as Gunnislake.

Thanks to the Dartington Amenity Trust the old port of Morwellham – pronounced MorwellHAM – has been largely restored so that a visit to this remarkable spot on the river will give anyone a good idea of the workings that went on here over 100 years ago.

In 1856 Queen Victoria, the Prince Consort and the Royal children landed at Morwellham on their way to visit the gardens at Endsleigh. From here they drove by coach along the Duke's drive to return to their steamer Gipsy later in the evening.

Morwellham was once the port to the manor house of Morwell which was owned and used as a retreat by the Abbot of Tavistock. The land was given by Henry VIII to the Russell family and later it became the loading place for all the minerals from the Great Consul Mines. It was a hub of activity during the mining days with its lime

The quay at Morwellham, once the scene of tremendous activity in the mining heyday of the nineteenth century.

kilns, corn mill, water wheels, incline planes and constant coming and going of ships. A new dock was built and the old houses were swept away to make room for the stock of ore and timber. The increased space meant there was room for 4,000 tons of ore on the tiled quay floors at any one time. The timber was taken to the saw mills at Wheal Josiah to shore up the huge underground spaces.

But although Morwellham was such a busy port it always remained a place for holidaymakers to visit or for a day's outing on the river.

I was lucky enough to be lent a friend's boat to go up the river from Plymouth to the now deserted harbour of Morwellham where we stopped for lunch. It was a still autumn day golden with sunshine and a robin came and sat on our picnicking table and literally shared our lunch from our plates.

I don't think there is a more wonderful way to spend a sunny balmy day than to travel up this great estuary by boat. The day we went, the river was as calm and flat as glass so that it seemed almost a shame to shatter the stillness with a noisy motorboat. It is hard to realise that this quiet greatness of water, cliffs, woods and grassy banks was once a busy industrial centre. No part of any modern motorway can have seen the diversity of traffic that once congregated on this waterway. Strange, too, that the countryside was filled with smoke from the great chimney stacks of the mines and the lime kilns. The smell was not too glorious when the dockyard dung was brought for manuring the fields. And yet because large areas of the valley belonged to the great landowners, the Bedfords and the Mount Edgcumbes, the countryside was protected and the damage done by the mines kept to a minimum.

So the valley, even in the busiest days of mining, remained a great beauty spot and the romantic paddle steamers made their way up the river to show off the banks of cherries, strawberries and bulbs that grew in profusion so close to the mines.

From Morwellham Quay you can take a little train that runs on the very edge of the cliff looking over the river and into an old disused mine. You can read and hear most things about the mining days of the Tamar valley without ever knowing what it was really like for this vast exploited workforce of miners who did the dirty work. But to enter the mine and feel and hear the drip of water from overhead and find yourself entombed in that damp eerie rock, makes it much easier to imagine the conditions these men worked under. I felt a kind of rage against man's inhumanities to his fellow beings.

And yet when we came out of the mine and I thanked the mining engineer who had driven the little train and explained things to us, I said I had never before had any inkling of what it felt like to be in a mine. 'No', he said 'any reconstruction of a mine is nothing short of an insult to the real thing.' I realised, not for the first time, that many miners, even those who worked under appalling conditions loved the mines and held them in great respect rather as a fisherman holds the sea. Neither mines nor the sea are to be trifled with but once you have learned to face them and work with them nothing apparently, compensates.

The project at Morwellham has grown to include many activities in the last eight years. Gary Emerson has been the director there for thirteen years and sees his job as 'conserving for the future elements of historic interest at the port'.

He wants to, and has indeed succeeded in, breathing life into the place as he finds that visitors are curious about the people who lived and worked at Morwellham. Morwellham has become of particular interest to organised educational groups. They can find out the intricacies which formed 'The Greatest Copper Port in Queen Victoria's Empire'.

In a nineteenth century cottage the port's smithy, cooper's workshop and assayer's laboratory have been fully restored and furnished. Workers there are dressed in the clothes of the 1860s and can answer questions about the type of life they would have been leading then. There is also a restored chandler's shop where goods on display are those which would have been sold there in the nineteenth century.

The farmyard has also been brought back to life with a farmer in period costume demonstrating a water powered threshing machine.

There are rides on the wagonettes pulled by shire horses which take visitors along the old Duke's Drive as well as the train rides along the side of the river bank and into the mine.

Most visitors to Morwellham Quay find such a variety of activities taking place that they will spend an average of four to five hours there. Shops are well stocked with many local goods and arts as well as a magnificent collection of history books relevant to the time when Morwellham was most active.

The latest project involves some replanting of orchards and a major interest in the horticulture that once was prevalent in the Tamar valley. The local artist, Mary Martin, who has a national reputation, is also much involved with crossing and rearing the original cherry and apple trees that grew in the Tamar valley and she has helped to replace some of these strains in the surrounding countryside.

There are about 160,000 visitors every year at Morwellham Quay though the place never seems to be overcrowded. There were fears that such a busy centre would ruin the Tamar river's present tranquility, but fortunately there seems to be no interference from the Quay. Tucked away as it is on the bend of the river neighbours are not unduly worried by the noise and activity. Traffic on the steep ascending hill road to the Quay is not congested.

It is well to remind ourselves that though many of us appreciate and try to guard the peace and quiet of the river it was not always as silent as most of the riverside places are now.

The decade between 1850 and 1860 was Morwellham's busiest time. Over 4,000 tons of copper ore would be lying on the quay awaiting shipment at any one time and 200 people worked and lived

A solitary truck stands on the abandoned railway at Morwellham.

in the little port with many people visiting.

Now there are 120 people employed part-time at the quay with 40 or 50 full-time employees.

The River Tamar played a major role in the mining history of the valley. The Duchy of Cornwall gave permission to the Devon Great Consols Mining Company to harness the waters of the Tamar to provide most of the basic power that was used in this most successful operation. It was partly due to this that the company made a profit of £300,000 between its beginning in 1844 and 1850. A huge amount of money at that time.

But what of those actually working in the mine? In a piece of research published in the Tamar Journal by the Friends of Morwellham and written by Christopher Taylor who was conducting a school project at Tavistock Comprehensive, we can learn much about the conditions of mining families in the area, many of whom lived along the banks of the Tamar river.

Wages were not paid at Devon Great Consols in the way we have come to regard as normal in our day. Wages were worked out according to a bartering method known as the 'tributing system'. It worked in the following way. The underground levels at the mine were divided into 'pitches' – stretches of ground where mining took place. The mine would be inspected from time to time by the managers or 'captains' as they were called, and then on a certain day in each month the miners would gather outside the count house at the mine. This was called 'setting day'.

The Clerk of the mine would describe each pitch in turn, and say how many men were needed to work each pitch for a certain length of time. The lowest bid for each pitch would win the right to work. The wages were low considering the size of the profits that were being made at the mine. In 1866 the average weekly wage for a miner was 14s 6d (73p) and the Bal Maidens – bal meaning mine in Cornish – who were the women workers got about 5p a day.

This can be considered alongside the price of groceries, for example tea was the equivalent of 20p a lb, sugar was about 5p for 2 lb and currants and raisins were about 5p a lb. A man who was earning just over £2 a week often had to provide for a family of five.

The mine employed a large number of young workers. Of the 1,230 employees in 1860 about 400 were children under the age of 13, some were as young as eight years old and many would have to walk four or five miles to work each day.

In 1859, a year in which the mine's shareholders were paid a dividend amounting to £45,000, the company put aside £100 to pay for a school at the mine for children of the miners.

Because of appalling accidents the miners were encouraged to put 1s 6d (7¹/2p) a month to a sick club for which they received 4s a week when they were too ill to work.

A form of trade union called the Miners Mutual Benefit was formed in 1865 when miners refused to bid for pitches at the mine on setting day. 120 extra policemen were called in from all over Devon to help control the situation at the mine. Meanwhile two companies of soldiers were sent from the army base at Devonport and held in reserve at the Bedford Hotel, Tavistock.

On March 3, the day designated for the strike, 2,000 people were gathered outside the count house. There was almost total silence. Only four of the pitches were taken; the mine was in danger of closing down.

However there were hundreds of miners out of work in the west of Cornwall. The Devon Great Consols Company drafted them in and

An old photograph captures the remnants of the once heavily industrialised Morwellham. By the time this picture was taken in 1906, Devon Great Consols Company, which kept the port so busy, had gone into liquidation.

they were so desperate for work that they took the jobs and the mine continued to produce copper. The striking miners were beaten and within a month most of them had returned to work.

But it was not long after this that the main copper lode was all but exhausted, added to which the price of copper was falling with the larger supplies becoming available from USA and Canada. In 1868 arsenic production was started at the mine and became the major money spinner. It was used in pesticides and in the chemicals industry as well as in the manufacture of glass, enamel, paints and dyes. Before long Devon Great Consols was producing half the world's supply of arsenic. But by 1899 the mine had begun to lose money and in November 1901 the company went into voluntary liquidation.

This had a devastating effect on the entire area. Many of the younger men went in search of work in Australia, Canada and Africa while most of the older men were never to work again. In 1861 the population of Tavistock was 8,965 but in the 1930s it had fallen to 4,500.

Calstock and Kit Hill

ROUND the great serpentine bend of the Tamar in which Morwellham is tucked you come to another old port at the town of Calstock. As Morwellham is built on the Devon bank, Calstock is its counterpart on the Cornish bank. Its houses are built on the steep slope, huddled together so that one terrace looks on to the roofs of the next.

Calstock was a river quay as long ago as Saxon times and in the 1400s its barges traded up and down river carrying sand, lime and granite moorstone. Tin was recovered at Kit Hill and Drakewalls above Gunnislake long before the Napoleonic wars. And until the coinage dues were abolished in 1838 it often served as a coinage town.

Kit Hill is a great landmark of the Tamar valley. So often looking up from the banks of the river you can see the great rounded hill topped by its famous chimney stack. As long as I can remember I have loved to walk on Kit Hill, and to see the panoramic view from its wild summit. I don't think there is a view in Cornwall to compare with it.

Kit Hill must be the most familiar landmark in the Tamar valley. Almost anywhere along the length of the river you can sight the rounded peak with its well known mine stack atop.

In 1895 when Prince Charles, Duke of Cornwall, announced the birth of his first son Prince William he gave the site of Kit Hill to the Cornish people. Though pleased with the gesture the local inhabitants of Callington district were somewhat surprised; they had always believed the hill to belong to them in the first place. It has long been a most popular walking place and wonderful vantage point to look out over a vast chunk of Devon and Cornwall. The views of the river Tamar are staggering and unique but choose a sunny bright day if you want to see it at its best. Kit Hill attracts the mists and fogs that are so much part of the Cornish weather and it is not all that often

In the 30s there was a considerable workforce at Kit Hill Quarry. Sporting caps and waistcoats these workers looked remarkably cheerful for the camera. Below, this photograph taken in 1934 gives an idea of the scale of quarrying carried out.

that vistas are far-reaching.

The hill now has its own ranger, David Powell, who has become an enthusiastic protector of this wild, stark bit of land. He is interested in every aspect of the hill and one bright February afternoon he and I walked around the peak as he told me something of the history that is involved. He combines his job of caretaker of Kit Hill with being warden of the Delaware Outdoor Education Centre.

The history of Kit Hill contains so much that is indigenous to Cornwall. Tin mining almost certainly went on there in a primitive form for centuries and there are archaeological remains of at least fourteen tumuli dating back to the bronze age. Recently a major survey has been carried out in the area revealing many new and ancient finds and a comprehensive report has been published by Cornwall County Council. Some of the facts will be republished in a smaller pamphlet form which will be available to all those who are interested in Kit Hill.

The mine stack itself epitomises much of the history of the hill, for there was mining of tin, copper, and later arsenic and much quarrying in the deep and awesome granite pit.

In the 1830s the stack was a windmill which was well known as a landmark in its time as the mine stack is now. The windmill supplied much of the power needed for the mines, as the steaming mine stack did later. Below the present stack lies a bastion of the pentagonal fort which dates back to the Civil War. It is believed that the Royalists held out here against the Parliamentarians. Below the fort lies a bronze age burial mound. Now the disused mine stack is covered in unsightly modern aerials used by the police and fire brigade.

The new plans for Kit Hill do not include any buildings. Local people have been most vociferous about their conception of the hill and how it should be kept as wild and unspoilt as possible. But there will be more organised parking places which will protect the surrounding land from erosion. There is to be a horse trail at the bottom of the hill and there are special plans for the enjoyment and education of the young in the area.

David Powell, who is an enthusiastic ecologist and environmentalist, is also very keen on energetic activities for which Kit Hill is a perfect setting. There are rock climbing facilities and the open spaces and rough terrain are excellent for adventure training. There are also some rare plants which will be well guarded.

It seems that history has been enacted out in the land around Kit

Hill so that it encapsulates much that is intrinsically Cornish and particularly part of the Tamar valley's past and present. That timelessness that is so apparent in the countryside around the river is most obvious here.

As children we were brought up playing on Kit Hill. My grandfather eulogised it, always telling us to take our friends there to see the 'finest view in the Kingdom'. It was only after he died that I realised that his special love for the peak was probably related to the fact that he became engaged to my grandmother on the top of Kit Hill.

In his little diary of 1901 I found the entry, 'Walked to the top of Kit Hill. Proposed to Eva. She accepted. This is a red letter day for me.'

I also discovered that the strange building called Kit Hill Castle on the south side of the hill was once owned by my great grandfather William Dingle who bought it as a convalescent home for those recovering from tubercolosis, a disease that was most prevalent in the nineteenth century. It was formerly an old mine engine house and in the Venning Postal Directory of 1901 I found the following entry: (Kit Hill castle) was many years since purchased by Mr W Dingle, Callington, who laid out a considerable sum in converting it into a residential house and the grounds, suitable for a health resort. It is 800 feet above sea level. It faces south, and from it very extensive views of Dartmoor, the river Tamar, and the surrounding countryside may be seen. The place is becoming every year increasingly popular, and visitors after staying there for a short time have been greatly invigorated and improved in health by the bracing and salubrious air of Kit Hill, and greatly enchanted by the scenery.

'Mr H. Medland, formerly of the Public Hall and Temperance Hotel, Callington, is the lessee, and has furnished apartments to let, or lodgings, all the year round, but in the summer season they are generally full, so it is necessary to make engagements early. This place has been strongly recommended for invalids by some eminent physicians and doctors, a few of whom have been there to stay themselves.' Now the building is privately owned.

In the 1700s Mr John Williams of Scorrier had bought the parish of Calstock and in the 1770s rich copper deposits were found and mined at the old Gunnislake mine proving most profitable for the Williams family, predecessors of Mr Rob Williams who I had visited earlier at Werrington Park.

In 1865 at least seventeen mines were working within five miles of Calstock and the slump in mining in the late 1800s caused terrible hardship in this area. By 1883 there were only two mines left working and the principal mining activity was arsenic. At this time the boast was that there was enough arsenic mined in the area to poison every man, woman and child in Britain.

But many other forms of activity went on at Calstock. There was the brick and tile making business, the papermaking, the brewery, a tannery, and most important, the shipbuilding yards. Calstock was always a tight, closely knit community and I have friends, who lived there until recently, who say this atmosphere still persists.

The great character of the shipbuilding world in the nineteenth century was James Goss. I went to meet his granddaughter, Phyllis, who still lives just above Calstock with her husband, Reginald Paige. He has just published a book about James Goss's life and work in the Tamar valley.

The view from the Paige garden down the Tamar valley is awe inspiring with the great grey rock of Morwell looking over the fir trees and sheer wooded slopes above Morwellham. They told me that they had come to live in Calstock during the war and had been lucky to find their bungalow, for in the terrible bombing days in Plymouth where they lived until their house was demolished as so many others were, Calstock had become a retreat for many suffering Plymothians.

They told me about the war years and how many people came from Plymouth each night seeking a quiet spot to rest their weary heads, unable to tolerate another night of bombing raids. Some people had been kind and taken those they could into their homes, others had been put up in Sunday schools and church halls and others had had to make do with chicken houses and pig sties. People had come, they told me, by train to Bere Alston and then walked down the hill through the woods to the Ferry Inn to catch the boat across the river to the village, their bed rolls under their arms, their tired children holding their hands. In the morning they would wend their way up the hill to the railway and back to Plymouth to carry out a day's work, view the devastation of the town and return once again in the evening.

Mrs Paige had given birth to her first son in the war years at Pentillie Castle. The Alexandra Nursing Home had been evacuated to the Castle for the duration of the war. 'We often used to tease my son when he was lazy – telling him he thought he could get away with anything just because he was born in a castle!' Mrs Paige told me laughingly.

The story of Mrs Paige's grandfather, James Goss, is quite a remarkable one. Wanting always to build ships of his own he had gone off as a ship's carpenter to Hong Kong, leaving his wife working at the Bealswood Brickworks. After two years and several unforeseen adventures, he returned; many had taunted his wife that she would never see her husband again but her faith in him was well founded. After his first eventful journey, when he had ended up in Australia, he took the shorter journeys to America until he had saved up enough money to rent from the Earl of Mount Edgcumbe the shipyard on the opposite side of the river from Calstock.

The skills of this craftsman have become a legend. He could not read or write but there was not a job in the shipbuilding yard that he could not do himself, filling in if any of his workmen went sick. He never marked the timber with a pencil but indicated measurements with a scratch of his thumb nail and his accuracy was never in question. In his shipyard, helped by his three sons, this remarkable man was busy all the year round building and repairing anything from ships of 150 tons to a skiff dinghy.

In the famous Calstock regattas, which were held from 1837 until 1937, there was always at least one member of the Goss family on the committee. The regatta was revived in 1967.

James Goss was not only a shipbuilder but he had such a gift with his hands that he could mend or make most things. When I went to visit Calstock Church with his granddaughter, she told me that he had been the only person able to repair the church clock at one time when it had been badly in need of attention.

It was the building of the Calstock viaduct in 1906 that was the end of the Goss shipyard. Once steam trains could travel over the river the boat traffic diminished and was soon gone. James Goss had been building his great ketch the *Garlandstone* – which is now restored and in dock at Morwellham – while the Calstock viaduct had been under construction, casting a shadow both real and prophetic across his famous boatyard. Mrs Paige told me that her father, Henry Goss, had never got over the going of the boatyard. Afterwards he had made a living by working the ferry and netting salmon but life had never been the same.

With the end of the mining and the river traffic Calstock became a much quieter town; hundreds of people in the area emigrated to America and other countries at this time and the whole atmosphere

A rather intriguing house at Calstock.

changed. Some of the emigrating miners were steerage passengers on the ill-fated Titanic.

R L Stevenson wrote in the later part of the nineteenth century in *Across the Plains* about his travels on the Central Pacific railroad line '...I had by this time some opportunity of seeing the people whom I was among ... There were no emigrants direct from Europe – save one German family and a knot of Cornish miners who kept grimly by themselves, one reading the New Testament all day long through steel spectacles, the rest discussing privately the secrets of their old-world, mysterious race. Lady Hester Stanhope believed she could make something great of the Cornish; for my part, I can make nothing of them at all. A division of races, older and more original than that of Babel, keeps this close, esoteric family apart from neighbouring Englishmen. Not even a Red Indian seems more foreign in my eyes. This is one of the lessons of travel – that some of the strangest races dwell next door to you at home.'

If you walk down beside the river from Calstock you will come to the unusual and famous hotel, now called the Danescombe Valley Hotel but once known as the Ashburton. One can imagine what a popular meeting place this must have been in the days when the river traffic was so busy. It has a second floor verandah and is built on the very edge of the water, looking downstream to the great mansion of the river, Cotehele. This area, Danescombe Valley, is named after the marauding Danes who are said to have fought a terrible battle here and made the valley 'flow with blood'.

Calstock viaduct, although surprisingly built of cement blocks instead of the granite so readily available in the area, is a most majestic sight especially when viewed from a distance. You can see it if you look down on the valley from a point just before Bere Alston or up the valley from Cotehele.

Looking up at it from Calstock towering above the town with its huge arches as it does, I longed to be on a train crossing over it. So one day I went with a friend on one of the prettiest train journeys imaginable. We caught the train at Plymouth which follows the river on the Devon bank to Bere Ferrers and Bere Alston and then crosses over the mighty viaduct at Calstock and finishes its journey at Gunnislake. But we remained on the train to travel back to Plymouth. The river views were so exciting it would have been a pity not to see them in both directions.

Some of the time the train travels through overgrown narrow

gorges and then, when least expected, the views open up and you can see for miles. I found it difficult to get my bearings at times for from the train the angles and perspective of views are totally different than from the road or from a boat, or when walking along the banks.

It was an experience not to be missed and one I hope to repeat often. The atmosphere on the train was so friendly – everyone greeting each other, the guardsman happily chatting to one and all and answering all our questions eagerly. It was as if we had travelled back to a time when the trains linked remote rural communities and were a joy to ride on not just a convenience to convey people from one great metropolis to another.

Cotehele

COTEHELE House, Quay and Mill are a complete world unto themselves. This was a community on its own recently working with buildings and machinery in complete use, but now kept by the National Trust as a reminder of all that went on here.

These are probably the most glorious wooded slopes of the Tamar. Here the oaks and beeches hang their branches in the river so that when the water recedes they are left with great tidemarks on their once glistening leaves.

Here the salmon fishermen come to cast their nets across the grand sweep of water, rowing their boats out to drop their nets then pulling them in hurriedly, sometimes happily catching vast salmon. It is hard work, needing skill and strength. To watch it is almost biblical in appearance, as old as time and, with its grand-scale movements and back drop of reflections and trees and boats, like a majestic ballet.

Here you can see the famous old barge the Shamrock now restored and on display at the Quay. A small museum in one of the old warehouses reconstructs the story of the river traffic and is a joint venture between the National Trust and the National Maritime Museum.

Up above the buildings of the Quay sits the romantic Tudor House. Its name comes from Hilaria de Cotehele who brought the house into the Edgcumbe family by marriage in 1353. And so it stayed Edgcumbe property until 1944 when the sixth Earl succeeded to the family estates and gave the House to the National Trust in lieu of death duties, the first time such a transaction had taken place.

The old Tamar river barge Shamrock, now restored to her former glory and moored at Cotehele Quay.

Medieval Cotehele House, home of the Mount Edgcumbe family and now in the care of the National Trust.

In 1533 the Edgcumbe family built their house Mount Edgcumbe on the parkland overlooking Plymouth Sound which still remains the family seat. This house was gutted by fire after being hit by a German incendiary bomb during the Second World War and the fifth Earl was forced to remove to Cotehele.

The glory of the house is a hundredfold. The grey granite, the courtyard, the great hall hung with armour, the kitchens with all the period utensils so polished and intact, the fine tapestries given with the house to the National Trust by the Edgcumbe family.

In the chapel is the clock installed by Sir Richard Edgcumbe in 1489. It is supposed to be the earliest clock in Britain still unaltered and in its original position. A pre-pendulum clock made entirely of wrought iron, it is mounted on a vertical oak beam and set on a shaft connected with a bellcote above which contained two bells. Until quite recently there were people who could remember the bell being sounded on the hour and ringing out over the woods surrounding Cotehele. When I took some Americans to see the house they remarked of the clock, 'So much better than a digital'. How right they were!

In 1988 on a cold February day with bright sharp sunshine my daughter was married in this little chapel. How honoured we felt to be able to see the simple yet moving marriage ceremony performed in the compact little chapel, each detail of it being so genuine and beautiful. I could have reached out my hand and touched my bridal daughter at any time during the ceremony. Only 60 guests could fit into the small building and we all sat very close together. It was somehow extra special that those people who most loved the bride and bridegroom should be so closely seated, in such an ancient atmosphere.

Cotehele's Mill House.

The quay at Cotehele was once a busy Tamar port.

What other ceremonies had happened in that building I wondered? What heartfelt prayers had been offered up? For so many years I had visited this house and chapel, walked in the gardens, eaten in the restaurant, shopped in the shop, sat by the river. It had become part of my life and the life of my family.

As a university student my daughter had come to work at Cotehele and she too had drunk up the atmosphere of the place, felt its own particular charm. Now at this important moment in her life she could be in a building we had always loved, somehow this added a dimension to the service, to the promises made and to the marking of a new stage in her life.

Past the snowdrops, under the great beech trees, she and her 'groom walked after the service to the reception held in the wonderful old barn. We filled it with white and yellow flowers, the colours of Easter, the time of promise for good things to come.

The gardens which slope so steeply down to the Tamar are a profusion of shrubs; azaleas, rhododendrons, fuchsias and many unusual trees. There is a lily pond, a dovecote in perfect condition

Abandoned winding gear at Cotehele Quay is a reminder of its
industrial past.

with the doves still making their home there although they are no longer used by the lords of the manor as fresh meat.

There is a bird's eye view from the terraces down the winding garden paths to the viaduct beyond at Calstock and a wide ribbon of river. If you walk down the steep garden paths and then follow the path towards the Quay there is another little chapel sitting on the precipice jutting out over the river. The story of the chapel is a particularly appealing one. In 1483 Richard Edgcumbe declared himself in league against the Crown. He was pursued by the local agent of the King, Sir Henry Trenowth of Bodrugan, who was much feared by the local residents. As he ran down the track by the river Richard Edgcumbe threw his cap into the water below. Trenowth and his men hearing the splash in the water and seeing only the cap left floating presumed that Edgcumbe was drowned. Thus he made his escape and eventually got away to Brittany.

But three years later Edgcumbe returned to build the chapel in thanksgiving and dedicated it to St George and Thomas a Becket.

The sequel to this story is that the terrible Trenowth had his estate confiscated by Henry VII who gave it to Richard Edgcumbe who in his turn chased his old enemy who actually jumped into the sea. A spot between Mevagissey and Dodman is now known as Bodrugan's Leap and is also owned by the National Trust.

The fascinating mill house up a little creek from the Quay was, until a short time ago, in full use. I have known for some time a remarkable character of this area. Mrs Marie Martin, whose father was the miller as his father had been before him. She talks about her childhood at the mill with clarity and happiness. It must have been a marvellous place to be brought up as there was always so much going on there.

The great trees were felled in the woods above and brought down to the mill to be sawn and cut. The grain was brought by horse and dray or up the river by barge, and unloaded at Cotehele Quay to be ground here. Some of the grain came from as far away as the River Plate. 'It was wonderful grain', Mrs Martin told me. 'I can remember our mother making popcorn from it.'

She can remember watching the men netting for salmon and the games she, her two sisters and her brother played by the river's edge. Her father had been one of thirteen children but, although he was the youngest son, he had taken over the running of the mill from his father who had made many improvements there.

Mary Martin country – the highly cultivated Tamar valley.

Marie Martin is a remarkable woman. She has a kind of aloof dignity that I have seen before in Cornish people, not taking to strangers easily but once she accepts them there could be no more generous friend. Although she has not often left the Tamar valley she is widely read, extremely knowledgeable and has a brilliant individualistic mind that stuns me when I talk with her.

She has always painted since she was a child and taken photographs. One of her paintings she showed me is a detailed picture of all the activities that went on at the mill when she lived there. There are the blue butterflies she remembers so clearly as part of life that are now extinct. The centre of the picture is the mother and baby. 'The newest baby was always the centre of life', she told me. There is Bill Roberts sawing the wood and dressing the millstone. She shows the horse and dray with sacks of corn, the yellow flags that grew by the river, the forget-me-knots, primroses and snowdrops, a bright kingfisher and the moorhen leaping from its nest on the river

71

bank. Here are the men bringing home the huge salmon netted on the Tamar and overhead a hot air balloon she remembers drifting past with people waving to the children below. She has depicted their barge, the Myrtle, later bombed in the estuary, and the men picking cherries from their high ladders – there were six or seven different kinds of cherries grown in the orchards above the mill. The great waterwheel turns and dragonflies flit here and there and, showing how cold one winter was, there are huge icicles hanging from the banks in one corner.

Mrs Martin, nee Marie Langsford, was born at the mill and was often told how one of the workmen had to ride by horse to get Doctor Leakey on the day of her birth.

Rent day at Cotehele had always been a great occasion with all the tenants going to pay their dues and having a midday meal with punch served from huge bowls at the house. It was a men-only occasion and they often came away slightly the worse for wear.

Mrs Marie Martin later married a farmer and went to live at Gooseford Farm, St Dominic. She had three daughters. Her youngest daughter Mary is also a very gifted painter and is most knowledgeable about this part of the Tamar valley. She attended the Royal Academy School in London and has since shown her paintings in many galleries and exhibitions all over the country.

She travelled through Europe when she left the Academy, but was always longing to get home to the Tamar valley which she loves so much. She knows the name of every field, all about the cherries grown on its banks and she has bunched flowers in a shed down by the river when the flowers were ready for picking from the south facing slopes of the market gardens above Cotehele.

She can often be seen, easel and canvas in hand, wandering through the lanes or standing amidst the bracken and wild flowers painting one of the scenes she knows, loves and depicts so well.

She has shown me marvellous secret places where the views of the river are most staggering and everyone we met while walking

The gifted painter Mary Martin at work alongside the Tamar.

seemed to be related to her in one way or another. Now she lives in an amazing little house she converted from an old stone barn belonging to her grandfather. It is like a tree house perched so treacherously on a hill above Glamorgan Mill among the trees. Her little house and a barn further up the valley belonging to her sister are literally bulging with her paintings, both oil and water colours.

Once I watched her painting a scene nearby on a hot summer's day with the flies pestering her and congregating around her head. When I asked her later if they had driven her mad she said she had not noticed them. When she is involved in her painting she forgets all else. She seems oblivious to everything except the view ahead and the paints on her palette.

In soft evening sunlight I have driven home from her barn having viewed her latest collection of pictures and each corner I turned in the lane seemed to offer up another one of her paintings. There is not a vista in this part of the valley that she has not painted at one time or another, so that sometimes it seems to me this bit of land between Cotehele and St Dominic entirely belongs to her.

But she would see it as belonging to the remarkable characters who have worked the market gardens and all the farms of this valley; growing the cherries that were famous all over the country, and the daffodils and anemones and strawberries. Some of this strip vegetation on the slopes to the river has disappeared, given over to evergreens or just left to run wild. The wonder is that it still exists in places, for the work on these steep inclines, is to say the least, back breaking.

'Narcissus Slope', one of Mary Martin's richly colourful paintings.

Halton Quay and
Pentillie Castle

A FEW miles downstream from Cotehele Quay the wide tidal river passes Halton Quay. This to me is the most magic spot on these last reaches of the river. I hate to write too much about it fearing that others will come to enjoy its tranquility and peacefulness that I, and others who live in the vicinity, treasure so much. To sit on the wall beside the water and watch the setting evening sun turn the water pink and bring a glow to the little chapel there and the Georgain row of cottages is a special treat for me. Not far up river there is a Holy Well at Chapel Farm which marks the spot where St Indract, son of an Irish King, his sister St Dominica and some companions landed in the seventh century and perhaps it is this special occasion that gives the place its unique atmosphere.

I love to go to Halton Quay at high or low tide. The shiny mud flats are full of bird life and have a charm of their own. The salmon fishermen come to net their salmon at high tide and this is another picturesque setting to see them perform their artistic deeds.

Just above Halton Quay is the manor house of Halton Barton. It was once a monastery and the story goes that there is a tunnel built between this house and Chapel Farm which was once a nunnery. Goodness knows for what reason, except that the monks might visit the nuns in secret!

The history of Halton Barton is full of myths and legends. It is said that once Sir Francis Drake fought with an admirer of his wife's from this house. And when the present occupants, Colonel and Mrs

The author Sarah Foot at Halton Quay.

Ferguson, bought the house in 1971 they were told that a red patch on their front doorstep was a bloodstain left from this encounter. They scrubbed at the red patch but each time it returned. Eventually they managed to scrape the mark away which Mrs Ferguson is sure was just the remnants of some red polish.

But there is the definite presence of a ghost in the house. Sometimes it shows itself merely as an ominous atmosphere of some spirit in the room, sometimes it is the sound of pacing, sometimes a shadow is seen passing in the passage.

In the sixteenth century the house was the home of Richard Carew's great friend, Anthony Rous, and in Carew's Survey of Cornwall he describes it thus: 'Halton the pleasant and commodious dwelling of Mr Anthony Rous both which benefits he employeth to a kind and uninterrupted entertainment of such as visit him upon his not spare inviting, or their own occasions, who (without the self guilt of an ungrateful wrong) must witness that his frankness confirmeth their welcome by whatsoever means provision, the fuel of hospitality, can in the best manner supply – and being yet scarcely entered the limits if an healthful old age, seeth his pedigree extended into two farther descents.'

It has a wonderful view down to the estuary and the stonework of the house and the mullion windows and old beams make it a beautiful house and one full of atmosphere. From the Quay you can look across at North Hooe Farm or downstream to Pentillie Castle Quay and its pretty boathouse.

Marie Martin's uncle used to be the coal merchant here at Halton Quay. They used to row down the river to see him or he would take them out on the river in his boat. There are the ruins of the old lime kiln and in the days of busy river traffic this quiet spot was once a hub of activity.

It provided easy access from Cornwall to the lead and silver mines around Bere Ferrers and so a ferry passed between the Cornish and the Devon banks. People living at Halton Quay could set their clocks by the bells of the count houses from the Devon mines opposite which marked the end and the beginning of shifts.

Pack horses brought granite from Hingston Down and much of the fruit and flowers grown on this fertile land were shipped downriver from this point. In 1926 the Quay was closed and became once again the peaceful secluded place it must have been when St Indract and his sister landed upstream in the seventh century. The quay is part of the Pentillie Estate and belongs to the Coryton family of Pentillie Castle.

A good alternative to walking the banks of the Tamar river is an exploration by paddling a kayak canoe along the tidal stretch of the river between Gunnislake and Halton Quay.

Ted Coryton of Tamar Canoe Expeditions encourages many people to do just this. He assures me that there is no need to be fit, or even to have canoed before, as the expeditions are timed to benefit from the helping hand of the tide.

Sarah Coryton and her son Oliver.

Everyone I have spoken to who has taken this canoe trip up the Tamar says it is an idyllic way to see the countryside and the wildlife. As you wend your way between the high wooded banks you can look up at the old mine stacks and imagine the time when the area was a bustling place with sailing barges like the Shamrock – well restored and resting now at Cotehele Quay – carrying goods up and down the river.

Ted and his wife Sarah take many parties of school children as well as social and youth clubs, some groups of mentally handicapped people, families and individuals – in fact anyone from eight to 80 years. The kayak canoes are extremely stable with wide open cock pits, a life jacket is provided and a safety boat follows every expedition at a discreet distance. You can choose whether to go in a single or double canoe.

Where the river froms a great horseshoe bend beyond Halton Quay high up in pride of place among some grand beeches and oaks sits Pentillie Castle.

The house was built in 1689 but the late Major Jeffrey Coryton told me it is believed there was a farmhouse and a chapel on the site before that date. It was built by Sir James Tillie who had originally been a steward to the Coryton family and had lived at Newton Ferrers on the Lynher since 1242. Eventually the great, great niece of James Tillie became heiress to Pentillie Castle and the estate and married a Coryton. Thus the house came to the Coryton family and it has remained theirs ever since.

Sir James Tillie, who died in 1712, was quite a character and commanded that when he died his body should be placed in a chair on a stone plinth at the top of Mount Ararat, a wooded hill facing the castle. He requested also that his pipe and his drink should be placed next to him. The monument still stands although his body was moved to a more conventional grave.

It was 1770 when the Coryton family became the owners of Pentillie Castle through marriage and in 1810 they carried out major alterations to the house changing the whole aspect. W. Wilkins was the architect who was also responsible for the National Gallery in London amongst other famous buildings.

The old lime walk which is the most beautiful sight is 200 years old and was once the main drive to the house, the two rows of trees being planted so close together that only one carriage could pass at any one time. To see the sunlight filter through these tall limes standing sentinel is one of the most glorious sights I have ever seen.

In 1965 Major Coryton came to live at the house on the death of his father. He had realised for some time that he would have to make the choice either to pull the old house down, as it was in such a terrible state of repair, or else to do some major reconstruction work. He and his wife decided on the latter and lived in a small flat in one wing of the house while the work was done. It was a major task and took four years from 1966 to 1970.

The house, as it stands now, is very similar to its original shape and size but is, if anything, even more beautiful. The simplicity of the front arches with their granite pillars cut from the quarry at Kit Hill and the sandy colour of the facing is unique and impressive. Sir James Tillie's statue stands in the front courtyard of the house surveying all

Pentillie Castle.

that goes on about him.

The house is now much more easily run and has somehow attained a new beauty, but it retains its old setting which must be one of the loveliest in Cornwall. And it is the Tamar that lends it the fine views and gives it such a special atmosphere.

The grounds lead down a steep wooded hill to the Quay with one of the finest outlooks of the river up to Halton Quay and across to the Devon banks. On one sunny morning I stood there and marvelled at this great last loop of the river. It seemed hard to believe that the little streams we had seen so far up to the north had become this massive wide sparkling river now spread out before me.

South Hooe Mine, Hewton House and Clifton House

AROUND this bend of the river up on the Devon banks lie the buildings at South Hooe Mine. Perched on the hill, the house that once belonged to the mine captain is now the home of my goddaughter Amy Dugmore and her family. The house has been completely renovated and down below the count house still stands, now completely rebuilt. You can see the large bay window from which the mine captain auctioned the pitches.

This was one of the richest silver mines in the country and was fortunate to have as its manager a gentleman by the name of Percival Norton Johnson. He became famous for his humanity and for the inventions he made to make the life of the miners easier, an unusual attribute among mine captains in those days. The richest lodes lay under the Tamar and to make it easier for the miners to get to these areas he built an incline shaft which meant they did not need to use ladders and were able to descend into the mine more easily. Many horrific stories are told of miners falling to their death as they climbed the great ladders out of the deep mines. They were often too tired to grip the rails tightly enough or place their feet surely enough on the rungs.

He also installed a fan ventilation system, so badly needed as many miners died at an early age from consumption. In 1852 over 200 people were employed in the mine. In 1866 Johnson died and the mine was never again so successful. 20 years later it was closed.

From this house one bright autumn afternoon I walked with my

The view from South Hooe Mine.

goddaughter and her mother along the top of the woods to Hewton House. I was interested to visit the house as Mrs Blanchard who had lived at Leigh Barton further up the river all her married life had been brought up at Hewton as a child.

Her life had always revolved around the river and she loved the view of the estuary from this point. Walking from South Hooe to Hewton one glimpses through the trees the remarkable vistas of the wide river as it spreads itself past Cargreen where the Tavy joins it.

Mrs Blanchard had told me how they often played among the old mines never realising the danger they were in. And they had thought nothing of rowing to Plymouth to go to the theatre and then rowing all the way back again in the early hours of the morning. As young children they had been taught to row and being in boats had been second nature to them, travelling by water to see people and places had been so much easier and nicer than travelling by road.

Hewton House is indeed a fine old house, added to over the years, the older parts being 400 years old. Mrs Woodford, who lives there now with her husband, came from the north. They have retired here and love the place. She kindly welcomed us and showed us the view from the patio, which looks down across the terraced gardens to Weir Quay below.

Weir Quay was one of the main loading places for ore in the mining days and the smelting works later became a famous jam factory. There are huge market gardens in this area, the south facing slopes affording wonderful positions for growing fruit, vegetables and flowers. The woods in spring between South Hooe and Hewton are a mass of sweet smelling flowering bulbs. This is also a favourite place for mooring boats and hundreds of sailing and fishing boats of every shape and size sit elegantly on this wide expanse of blue.

From South Hooe Mine you look across the river to Clifton House on the Cornish banks. Once this was a manor house where the Lower family lived for many years. Now nothing remains of the mansion but the cottages there were built from the stone of the old house. Leslie Spence, the artist, lives there now with his family but the property is part of the Pentillie Estate.

In 1636 Theodore Palaeologus, who claimed to be the last descendant of the medieval Christian Emperors of Byzantium, died there, and was buried at Landulph Church which is situated in a small creek further down the river. In 1962 the Queen and Prince Philip visited the church to see the tomb of Palaeologus of whom

Prince Philip is a descendant.

The poet and writer Barbara Walker, who lives on Ziggarson Hill just above Landulph wrote this poem about the Queen's visit on the day:

The hill, the wood, the stream –
This is the scene:
These are the noises;
The cooing of the pigeons wooing
And our chattering voices.

Won't be long now'.
Still, when you're talking the time don't drag'.
All in our clean frocks we sat on the wall;
I carried a green bough,
Mrs Rundle a flag,
and the rest had nothing at all.

'Listen! They're coming. Must be her this time'.
The out-rider; the escort ... 'There, that's it!'
The car with the crown on!
Hog-weed and meadow-sweet sway down;
We wave:
She gestures but her face is grave.
Her head is capped with white flowers.
The Prince sits beside her.
They are gone.

Gone, gone! There has gone a mystery.
How brief a look
We had upon the flying book
Of history!
'A drop of thunder-rain'.
We laugh, chatter again.
Then scatter.
What does it mean?
Shall we remember in a dream
This time and place,
The fluid curtsy of the grasses
When a Queen passes?

The Lower Reaches
of the Tamar

JUST a short way up the Tavy, a tributary which joins the Tamar here, lies one of the most romantic churches in Devon. Bere Ferrers church is built right on the water's edge and reminds me of another riverside church, St Winnow. It is surrounded by the churchyard of grey slate and granite gravestones and the river seems to lend it a special peacefulness.

I feel particularly attached to this church for my family were living in Bere Ferrers when I became engaged and the banns of my marriage were read here. Twenty years later we came, one bright Christmas morning, to witness my goddaughter Amy Dugmore who lives at South Hooe Mine being christened and later in 1988 on Easter Day another goddaughter Tatiana Cutts was christened there – her family live at Bere Barton in the village of Bere Ferrers – so it is full of happy memories for me.

The name of the village comes from Bere, the Celtic word for peninsula, and Ferrers was the name of the Lord of the Manor who was a cousin of William the Conqueror. The setting of the church is wonderful and the interior is no disappointment. It has a rough Norman font of great beauty and in the eastern window is some of the oldest stained glass in Devon. It has just undergone major renovation.

Cargreen village is built on the Cornish bank almost opposite the point where the Tavy comes to meet the Tamar. The main street runs straight down to the river and in the seventeenth century Richard Carew described it in his Survey of Cornwall as a 'fisher town, but can hardly muster a mean plight of dwellings or dwellers'. Things have changed since those days and now too many people want to build at this lonely headland and the local residents are hard put to defend their little town from over population.

**Looking down on the twin road and rail bridges over the Tamar at
Saltash.**

For years Cargreen was one of the central points of the market
garden industry and it was here the fruit and vegetables were brought
to be loaded onto the ferry that took them across the river. The
produce was then carried up the hill to meet the railway line at Bere
Alston. The innkeeper doubled as ferryman and the inn still stands at
the end of the main street but now it attracts holidaymakers and
many local people from villages and towns round and about. It no
longer performs the task of quenching the thirst and hunger of those
who worked so hard in the area.

One day I walked with a friend, at low tide, along the banks of the
river from Cargreen to Salter Mill. It is a quiet unspoilt part of the
country. The views across to the Devon banks are marvellous and

this is a favourite spot for bird watchers. It makes it all the more understandable that once Tony Soper, that famous bird man, lived at Salter Mill. It is a very secluded hamlet with two houses once lived in by farm labourers of the Pentillie Estate.

We stopped there to talk to friends and take a cup of tea and then found that our return journey had been entirely cut off by the rising tide. It was a good reminder of the importance of the changing tide. Those rowing on the river always make sure they are going with the tide or else the journey can become almost impossible as I have learned to my cost. In fact all the activities on the river are governed by the tides and the beauty of the river is increased by the changing face the ebb and flow lend it.

Below Cargreen the river passes the parish church of Landulph where Palaeologus is buried and beyond there is a deep creek and the house of Moditonham. *Murray's Handbook for Devon and Cornwall* which was printed in 1859 says that this is 'the house in which the Commissioners of the Prince of Orange treated with the Earl of Bath for the surrender of the castles of Pendennis and Plymouth'.

The house is now owned by the National Trust but once it was part of the Valletort's estates. They were the Lords of Trematon Manor and from 1871 until about 30 years ago the Loam family lived there. In the last war a bomb was dropped in the courtyard and ruined a large part of the old building. At the quay a wall was built to prevent the water from the Tamar coming too high and two fields were reclaimed from marshland.

From Moditonham Quay the river widens to lakelike proportions as if to show off its full extent of beauty before passing under the two bridges of Saltash; Brunel's famous railway bridge and the majestic modern toll bridge.

Saltash is a much older town than Plymouth.

> *Saltash was a borough town*
> *When Plymouth was a furzy down*

So the old song goes. But sadly this old town has been swamped by modern development and is in danger of losing its character and becoming merely a dormitory for the ever-growing city of Plymouth.

Saltash was famous as a fishing town and apparently the women of the town were in the habit of winning many of the prizes in the famous local regattas. It was also the home of Sir Francis Drake's

A very different face of the river is shown at Devonport.

wife, Mary Newman.

Carew tells us that in the sixteenth century the town had 'a mayor and ten brethren and possesseth sundry large privileges over the whole haven, to wit, an yearly rent of boats and barges appertaining to the harbour, anchorage of strange shipping, crowning of dead persons, laying of arrests, and other admiral rights, besides electing burgesses for the parliaments, benefit of the passage, for-closing of other save themselves from dredging of oysters except between Candlemass and Easter . . .' Carew had been a Member for Saltash in the Parliament of 1584-1585.

But by 1749 the Burgesses were claiming jurisdiction over the

A tug heads towards Devonport.

whole river as far as Calstock. The heavy tolls they were demanding led to a storm of protest. The leader of the opposition was none other than James Tillie from Pentillie Castle. Mr Tillie having secured alliance with the Governor of Plymouth published a manifesto in 1759 telling the masters of the ships to pay 1s for buoyage and no more to Saltash. He won his case and said, 'so that now the Gentlemen of the River are entirely free from all encroachments of the unjust and iniquitous Saltashers'.

The ferry that used to run at Saltash was a very ancient institution and is documented as early as the thirteenth century but was used as a crossing point long before that. It belonged to the Manor of Trematon and in 1356 the Black Prince, first Duke of Cornwall and Lord of Trematon, rewarded his porter William Lenche for his good service at the Battle of Poitiers – during which he had lost an eye – by giving him the lease for life of the Passage of Saltash.

I can remember so clearly waiting as a child when coming home to Cornwall from Plymouth for the ferry to arrive at our side of the river. It was often late at night and we were tired bundles in the back of the car but we woke to watch the glinting lights of Saltash beckoning. Once embarked on the crossing, I loved the sound of the water brushing the side of the ferry, the clunk of the chains and to get out of the car and feel the wind on my face and to look up at those great arching tubes of the Brunel bridge looming out of the darkness. Now when we cross the new toll bridge my father says it is like entering the Gates to Paradise. But it does not hold the same magic for me as crossing on the water.

To see these two bridges at their best the place to be is on the water in a boat. From some distance below the bridges as you wend your way through the battleships, the two very different styles form a marvellous pattern.

It took ten years to build the rail bridge designed by Isambard Kingdom Brunel, and it was one of the engineering feats of the Victorian Age. By the time it was finished Brunel was on his death bed. The scene I would most like to have witnessed was the day when the central girders were floated into position on the rising tide. Brunel conducted the proceedings from a platform mounted high on the central truss and he had insisted that the whole operation be carried out in complete silence.

A huge crowd had gathered to see the great event. Brunel's biographer describes the scene, 'there fell a dramatic stillness like that which follows the tap of a conductor's baton, and every eye in the vast crowd was strained towards the distant figure of the engineer. Numbers whose purport was unintelligible to the crowd were displayed; flags flickered and then the huge truss swung slowly and majestically out into the Tamar. 'Not a voice was heard', wrote an eye witness, 'as by some mysterious agency, the tube and rail, borne on pontoons, travelled to their resting place, with such quietude as marked the building of Solomon's temple. With the impressive silence which is the highest evidence of power, it slid, as it were, into position without an accident, without any extraordinary mechanical effort, without a misfit, to eighth inch'.

But when Prince Albert came to open the bridge in 1859 Brunel was not there. When he took his last look at the completed bridge he was a very sick man. He lay on a specially prepared platform truck while one of Gooch's locomotives drew him slowly beneath the pier arches and over the great girders.

On the day I went up the river by boat it was wonderfully exciting to pass under those two great bridges and enter the large lake-like entrance to the river. Past the barges holding large quantities of ammunition and past their rather sinister tunnels going into the rock face of the hill on the Devon banks where ammunition is stored. Then speeding through the sheet glass silver water towards the narrower entrance that was to take us up to so many lovely places. On that day this wide expanse of water seemed like open arms gathering us in to lead us up the river.

Now coming down the river and realising that this was the final end of my journeying this wideness once again reminded me of open arms, but this time opening to let me free, to go my own way.

But the wonder is that I need not say farewell to the river. For living as close to it as I do I can go in search of the many places along its banks that have become such favourite sanctuaries. Hardly a day passes that I am not in sight of the river but happily I do not grow accustomed to it. Each time I cross the toll bridge I am aware of that wide, watery divide with its many moods. In the same way I can never drive or walk close to the higher reaches of the river Tamar without a sense of home-coming and of familiarity.

Now that I have discovered so much of the river's history I often wonder what strange and interesting pastimes and actions will take place in the future on or along the banks of the river? Happenings that will in their turn become part of the river's story.

Certainly learning about the river, reading of the lives of the fishermen, miners, farmers and market gardeners and talking to their relatives and inheritors I have found a new dimension and come a little closer, perhaps, to understanding the universal pattern of the past, the present and the future.

Bibliography

Tamar Valley Traveller
by Joan and Terry Doyle
Published by Cornish Safari Company

Old Cornish Bridges and Streams
by Charles Henderson and Henry Coates
Published by Bradford Barton, Truro

Along the Bude Canal
by Joan Rendell
Published by Bossiney Books

A Shell Guide of Cornwall
by John Betjeman
Published by Faber

Legends of Cornwall
by Sally Jones
Published by Bossiney Books

A Shadow from Light Drifting
by Barbara Walker
Published by Ziggarson Company, Botus Fleming,
Saltash, Cornwall

Other Bossiney titles include . .

THE BARBICAN
by Sarah Foot
Thoughtfully combines words and old photographs, many appearing in book form for the first time.
'Having read this I can't wait to explore the Barbican again . . .'
June Glover, The South Hams Group of Newspapers

FOWEY – RIVER AND TOWN
by Sarah Foot
An enlarged and updated edition of Following the River Fowey.
'The intricate tapestry of this delightful area is woven together with warm, understanding interviews . . . buy, beg or borrow it.'
The Cornish Times

MYSTERIOUS PLACES
by Peter Underwood
Visits locations that 'seem to have been touched by a magic hand'. The man who has been called Britain's No. 1 ghost hunter reflects: 'We live in a very mysterious world . . .'
'. . . an insight into some of the more mysterious places in the south west.'
David Elvidge, Launceston & Bude Gazette

MYSTERIES IN THE DEVON LANDSCAPE
by Hilary Wreford & Michael Williams
Outstanding photographs and illuminating text about eerie aspects of Devon. Seen on TSW and Channel 4. Author interviews on DevonAir and BBC Radio Devon.
'. . . reveals that Devon has more than its share of legends and deep folklore.'
Derek Henderson, North Devon Journal Herald

MY CORNWALL
A personal vision of this Celtic land by Daphne du Maurier, Ronald Duncan, James Turner, Angela du Maurier, Jack Clemo, Denys Val Baker, Colin Wilson, C. C. Vyvyan, Arthur Caddick, Michael Williams and Derek Tangye.
'An ambitious collection of chapters.'
The Times, London

We shall be pleased to send you our catalogue giving full details of our growing list of titles for Devon, Cornwall, Somerset, Dorset and Wiltshire as well as forthcoming publications. If you have difficulty in obtaining our titles, write direct to Bossiney Books, Land's End, St Teath, Bodmin, Cornwall.

Plus . . .

LEGENDS OF CORNWALL
Sally Jones

GHOSTS OF CORNWALL
Peter Underwood

DARTMOOR IN THE OLD DAYS
James Mildren

COASTLINE OF CORNWALL
Ken Duxbury

DISCOVERING BODMIN MOOR
E. V. Thompson

PLYMOUTH IN WAR AND PEACE
Guy Fleming

SUPERNATURAL ADVENTURE
Michael Williams

UNKNOWN DEVON
Rosemary Anne Lauder, Michael Williams & Monica Wyatt

E. V. THOMPSON'S WESTCOUNTRY

THE CRUEL SEA
David Mudd

DART — THE MAGICAL RIVER
Ken Duxbury